DAYLIGHT SAVINGS

Steven Bauer

DAYLIGHT
SAVINGS

STEVEN BAUER

Peregrine Smith Books
Salt Lake City

First edition

92 91 90 89   5 4 3 2 1

Copyright © 1989 by Steven Bauer

Published by Gibbs Smith, Publisher, P.O. Box 667, Layton, Utah 84041. This is a Peregrine Smith Book

Design by Smith & Clarkson

Printed and bound in the United States of America

Library of Congress Cataloging-in-Publication Data

Bauer, Steven, 1948-
    Daylight savings / by Steven Bauer.
      p.   cm. (Peregrine Smith Poetry Series : v. 3)
    Poems.
    ISBN 0-87905-322-4
    I. Title.
PS3552.A83644D3   1989   88-39566
811'.54 – dc19   CIP

The paper used in this publication meets the minimum requirements of American National Standard for Information Sciences – Permanence of paper for Printed Library Materials, ANSI Z39.48-1984. ∞

FOR ELIZABETH ARTHUR

ACKNOWLEDGEMENTS

Grateful acknowledgement is made to the following pub-
lications in which some of these poems have appeared,
many in earlier form: *Ascent*, "In The Catskills" (from
"Four for Thomas Cole"); *Chariton Review*, "Heat Light-
ning," "Stopped in Memphis," "Raid on the Inarticulate,"
"Tornado Watch"; *Chicago Review*, "In Canaan," "Plugging
in the Flowers"; *Cimarron Review*, "Obsessive Reworkings
of the Same Theme"; *Dacotah Territory*, "Fifth Grade";
Denver Quarterly, "Lust," "Seals in the Damariscotta,"
"Twins"; *Gritloaf Anthology*, Palaemon Press, "Reclaiming
the Family"; *High Plains Literary Review*, "Digging the
Grave," "Reading"; *Indiana Review*, "Evening";
Massachusetts Review, "Between Two Oceans," "Marconi
Station: South Wellfleet"; *Missouri Review*, "Hint of
Spring"; *MSS.*, "Bug Sprayer," "Music"; *The Nation*,
"Stars in Maine"; *Oxford Magazine*, "Out Here"; *Poetry
Now*, "Mobilgas," "Ring-Necked Pheasant"; *Prairie
Schooner*, "Aspen Grove: New Mexico," "Daylight
Savings," "Naming the Shells," (under the title "Dead
Shark at Long Nook,") "Grass," "Intro to Poetry," " 'The
Man Who Knew Too Much,' " "Vagrant"; *Seattle Review*,
"Japanese Beetles"; *Southwest Review*, "White Cedar
Swamp."

The quote in *Japanese Beetles* is from the noted scientist
J. B. Haldane.

I am indebted to Christopher Merrill, Hilda Raz, Michael
Rosen, Liz Rosenberg, David Schloss, and Jason Shinder
for their encouragement, support, and help in completing
these poems. Thanks as well to the Fine Arts Work Cen-
ter in Provincetown and the Indiana Arts Commission.

CONTENTS

• • • • • • • • • • • • • • • • • • • •

Intro to Poetry   *xiii*

I.
White Cedar Swamp   *3*
Twins   *4*
Fifth Grade   *5*
"The Man Who Knew Too Much"   *6*
Reclaiming the Family   *7*
Bug Sprayer   *8*
Ed Sullivan Begins the Sixties   *9*
Grass   *10*
Daylight Savings   *12*

II.
Raid on the Inarticulate   *15*
Mobilgas   *16*
In the Catskills   *17*
Obsessive Reworkings of the Same Theme   *18*
Lust   *19*
Japanese Beetles   *20*
Music   *21*
Vagrant   *22*
In Canaan   *24*

III.
Reading   *27*
Digging the Grave   *28*
Hint of Spring   *29*
Old Faithful   *30*
Heat Lightning   *31*
Tornado Watch   *32*
Evening   *33*
Marconi Station: South Wellfleet   *34*

IV.
Stars in Maine   *37*
Between Two Oceans   *38*
Stopped in Memphis   *39*
Out Here   *40*
Ring-Necked Pheasant   *41*
Aspen Grove: New Mexico   *42*

Naming the Shells   43
Seals in the Damariscotta   44
I Bet   46
Plugging in the Flowers   47

INTRO TO POETRY

· · · · · · · · · · · · · · · · · · · ·

You thought it was math that taught
the relation of time and speed,
but it's farther than you knew
from that sunlit white-walled classroom
to this darkened lounge with its couch
and overstuffed chairs. How many miles,
would you say, since we talked
as if poetry were no distorting mirror,

one-way street? But listen: sometimes
it's like this, a stranger's Ford pulls up
and you, with no plans for the afternoon,
get in. He doesn't talk, stares at the road
and it's miles before you understand
you didn't want to travel. His lips say *no*
as you reach for the radio's knob.

In this silence, you fall deeper
into yourself, and even the car
disappears, the stranger's face blurs
into faded upholstery, and all things
being equal, you're alone as though
you've wandered into a forest with night
coming on, no stars, the memory of sun
and a voice asking *Is this my life?*

WHITE CEDAR SWAMP

From the sea the trail snakes down through
  sassafras and pine, and as I go my fingers
    crush the oily mitten-shaped leaves and tapered

needles until I smell of root beer, turpentine,
  and pitch. I walk here once a week, a connoisseur
    of change, to see what's different: the new blunt

buds the swamp maple jabs at winter, another trunk
  tattooed by lichen, or the poofy brown-and-white
    unraveling of punk. But as the ground defers

to water, the trail to raised and weathered planks,
  I see again that here, nothing changes: the clear
    tea-colored water sifting its fraying deciduous carpet,

collars of ice restraining the eelgrass hammocks,
  the darting bright-eyed agitation of a waxwing,
    and over all, the evergreen fragrance of the cedars

fanning the aqueous light through their spatulate
  fingers. If I stand still I can hear the constant
    question of the ocean, and the land's broken reply:

almost like learning to wade, but tripping, falling,
  submerged, still touching bottom, before being pulled head-
    long into a wall of surf which never stops. My father took

my hand when I was a boy and helped me into the waves,
  then telling me to trust him, held me by my ankles above
    the whole white water-topped world; said *Don't be afraid.*

TWINS

· · · · · · · · · · · · · · · · · · ·

In the numbness of our first room
I turned to him and said,
This is how we will always be,
then huddled closer in the dark
and tried to touch. We tumbled

into sense, the slap of air,
a hum of voices screened by glass,
and lay beside each other. On his face
a thinner mouth and greener eyes,
a paleness to the cheeks like early frost.

I slept, and in my dream reached out
a hand curled slowly to a fist,
and waking, found myself alone.
And growing, walked through every day
looking for a face which wasn't mine

but was. For years I've searched
the buildings of my life
for premonitions of the final room
where I'll discover him, alone
and shuttered in an oaken chair.

I want him back. I need to talk to him,
to learn why words were never spoken in return,
why he withdrew when I moved closer in my sleep
before the sun rose and I circled,
an exiled planet in the dark.

FIFTH GRADE

· · · · · · · · · · · · · · · · · · · ·

My teacher is pregnant.
When I wake considering that stomach, when I ask,
my mother has meals to cook and beds to make,
she can't believe I'm old enough. That spring, as May
conjures the sheaths of skunk cabbage from the swamp,
she drives the maple-bowered streets, new leaves
now straining into view, and stands a distance

from the playground to observe our play. She sees
it's not just me: we're all a little strange—
the boys still hugging boys, then wrestling in the mud
but with a roughness now, a wariness, not tender,
not a bit, then staggering to our feet
abashed, as girls, a gaggle of them,
giggling, walk by. A hotness

in her cheeks as from a slap. Back home
she thumbs the fraying collar of a shirt
in which she's sewn my name, closes a closet
on my broken toys. She opens up the scrapbook
to a house, blue-crayoned, with a simple sun,
a mother, father, and a little boy. Then she stands
cradling my name, waiting for the bus

to bring me home. When I descend, watching
Melissa Gleason walk away, she understands
I've grown so far from her, it isn't me
she's watching. She looks to the sky for a rainbow,
a flaming sword, but clouds are thighs
or buttocks. And though she wants to hold me, stop me,
lock me in, there's nothing she can do to keep us.

"THE MAN WHO KNEW TOO MUCH"

Insulted by the rain in Hackettstown,
my stormy father slouches, hands
thrust through his pockets to his thighs.
I pull his sleeve, lean against the brick,
stare at the flashing marquee.
It's a mystery he tells me, kicking
litter in the gutter's grey water.

The boy ahead of me in line
befriends me, squirts me in the eye
from a plastic flower on his lapel.
What's a little extra water?
my father says, and pulls me to his side.

He's so tall the rain gleams
in his hair; his hands are deeply smudged
from newsprint and from oil.
It must be my fault then, his silence,
the way he covers up his hairline with his coat.

Of course the kidnapped son is rescued.
When the lights come up, the floor
around my father is a field of popcorn.
Outside, the rain's intensified, and though
I squint both up and down the sidewalk,
I can't find my friend. All the way home
I wait for the explanation, but the smooth
shush of the wipers tells me Qué
será, será, that's all he has
to say on the subject.

RECLAIMING THE FAMILY

· ·

The pleasant meadowland I came from
turns to swamp. Father's never home,
Mom's at the store, and all my brothers
and sisters are off somewhere—at Little League,
in tree forts, at competing malls. Each day
the TV starts at noon and doesn't stop

till midnight. Something must be done.
I build wings for myself, fly around
the rec room like a bat. "Help," I say,
"I need some help," but who else cares?
When I leave the house I find my mother
in a Food Mart overcome by choices,

hypnotized by sales I hardly understand.
Campbell's Soup, for instance. I hover
as she places can after red can in her basket.
This must be stopped, I think, and yet I'm
scared to tangle in her hair. When she steps
on the magic carpet of the "Out" door

I fly out too, and all the way home
I know what I must do. That night
the house is dead, the last newscaster
fades to grey. Downstairs in his chair
my father snores the night away. I hoist him
on my back, flap up the stairs. I place him

at my mother's side, then swoop over my siblings,
whisper pleas through sheets they've pulled
above their heads. When they won't come I drag them,
line them up like sandbags beside our parents' bed.
"Help," I say, "I need some help." But it's all done.
The swamp has been reclaimed.

We're all together at last.

BUG SPRAYER

. . . .

It's still as death, my mother says,
our back porch on summer evenings
before the tree frogs open their throats.
I linger over lima beans, my father
stares at my plate, at me chewing
so slowly I think the world will stop

when we hear a noise from the next block
like an uncocked hydrant spraying
the sky, but it isn't water, I know that sound
better than breathing, it's a glorious yellow
truck with cylindrical tanks and nozzles
sticking from the back like teats. It turns

the corner to Elmwood Road and lays down
a thick white blanket of smoke, rolling
over the clipped lawns to the porch
so sweet and strong my father gives up
and I'm out the door and on the street
where all the neighborhood kids

are running, feet beating the pavement, hands
over our mouths. The driver leans out
his window and yells, but nothing stops us,
not the parents who list from screen doors
calling our names, the threat of a whipping,
parked cars looming from the fog.

It's heaven, this cloud of DDT
boiling like dry ice, this world
where everything common is changed—
my street, our neighborhood's white toy houses.
I shout through the whirling air,
seeing nothing, about to pass out,

I run exultant into the poisonous smoke.

ED SULLIVAN BEGINS THE SIXTIES

Our placid living room condenses to a square
wood box and variations on a theme of greys.
Even now, across two decades, I can see
my brother on his belly. His young chin sways
on his palms, his legs splay to a careless V.
At fourteen, almost an adult, I choose a chair

and join my parents, sedate in Sunday bliss,
the whole suburban family settled back.
Bombarded by the soft electrons' hiss,
we watch the swinging chimps, the sullen No-Doz
funny man, the Rumanian juggling act,
the elephantine opera diva. Then through his nose

our stiff-necked host stutters a few words,
sweeps back his rigid arm, and the camera dollies
to four black-suited baby-faced mop-haired guys
not much older than I. Knock-kneed, leering, alive,
they grip their electric guitars amid the absurd
commotion the girls are making and start to holler.

So surprised am I that my heart, that clenching fist,
pounds loudly against my ribs, and my eyes
accustomed to hooded languor, open wider than wide.
If I weren't so completely bedazzled, I'd twist
to my feet and shout, but my instincts advise
dissemblance: *now* I've got something to hide.

The thin wedge of my mother's face
turns to my father beside her and speaks
with rasping scorn. I can barely keep my hands
from rushing to clamp her mouth in place,
silencing all three of them for a week
of Sunday nights. I need time. My glands

without any attempt to obtain my go-
ahead have gone recklessly into overproduc-
tion, as though I've been shot from a cannon
into inner space. Everyone better hold on.
This is my family's, my country's bad luck.
I can feel it. My hair is beginning to grow.

GRASS

· ·

In late afternoon, the bell
of the Waterville Baptist Church
disappears in a blaze of falling sun.
From across the street I can smell

the grass caught in the mower's blades,
ripped loose and flung against the wall
of summer air. The teenage kid is naked
to the waist, as tall, as unafraid

as I those August nights past supper, swearing
before my parents' expansive lawn.
It was the summer of sixty-six. Later,
the guys would drive by, the radio blaring,

a case of Bud in the back, a lit smoke
in every mouth. I couldn't wait. But right
at that moment, the bugs coming out,
my only concern was the choke

of the mower's starter. I was goddam *there:*
I didn't remember my childhood, the swamp
where I'd skewered bullfrogs with a stick,
the girl two houses down whose bare-

ly rounded breasts were the first I'd seen.
I didn't yet know what Nixon could do
with scarcely six years and a nation's
confidence, nor had I been

transfixed by gas and the bright bayonets
in D.C. I was just a kid with a thirst
for beer and fast cars; my hair was still dark,
my spine intact, no deaths, not yet.

I adjusted the throttle, and cut the grass.
I pushed the mower in smaller and smaller squares.
I listened as the motor coughed itself to silence.
Mosquitoes, a barking dog, the lingering smell of gas.

Soon Cal and Don would drive up, already half-gone,
"Like a Rolling Stone" on the box. I stooped,
took a handful of grass. It smelled to me like the future
which seemed at the time, well, like anyone's.

DAYLIGHT SAVINGS

Seven-thirty, last weekend in April,
the sun, like a laggard child, still thumbs
the greening branches
to see how new the world's become.
In this light it's hard to admit so little
has changed. *Maria,* I say, *kiss me.*
When she does, I give myself up
to the pollen
falling from the light-streaked clouds,
tulips holding their white chalices open
to the air. I remember that first evening

I was freed after supper,
amazed by the extra light,
the flat planes of houses aflame
with a radiance I'd never notice again.
The moon hung in the sky, a pale promise.
I hid beside the house, the maple
with its new leaves, green stars
gathering the darkness,
my mother on the red brick steps
cupping her mouth and I thought

I have light, I have light
in my pockets, I'll save it.

II.

RAID ON THE INARTICULATE

. . . .

In their village words are stolen
from the children's mouths
before the first howl.
Their warriors travel
to our territory and gather
all we have said,
hanging in the air like smoke
or fallen underfoot.

This is a tale the elders tell
when embers burn to ashes and the dark
claps our ears like a shell
roaring the inexpressible.

We have been taught to hate
these people who grunt
and snuffle,
to fear them as roebucks fear tigers,
the elders death. Soon they will dam

all streams leading to our village
and the fish will gasp on the still beach,
opening and closing their mouths,
no sound.

We are girding for battle. My brothers
scratch their faces with roots, tie
bones in their hair, for bone
is the totem of *word* and the captives
will rise to the stockade's top
and wait for us. I am going too.

We are going tomorrow when the sun
touches the forest's lip.
We are walking. The women
are coming with us, they sharpen
spears they will carry, they sharpen teeth.

We are going on a journey.
We are going to bring back the words.
We have things to say.

MOBILGAS

· ·

after Edward Hopper

A man stands in the luster
of summer dusk, woods massed
and silent at his back.

He's swept the bare cement
so clean the station seems abandoned.
In the presence of that army of pine

he polishes the thick red pumps,
he counts the shining oil cans
resting in their metal stand.

He'd like to leave, but he's forgotten
where the light switch is,
and like a dream, an Oldsmobile may come.

Fill her up? he'll ask, standing
for patient hours at the tank
and it will never overflow—

It's 1940. In the dying light
the red winged horse strains upward,
waiting for the war to start.

IN THE CATSKILLS

after Thomas Cole

Summer filters through the air
like gold dust, touching with a brush
the ordinary weeds. The trees here
feather in the spring, remain ethereal. Nature
has no edges, the pastel mountains fade to sky,
each detail glides into itself and silently out
of another.

           This place where men chase stallions
through a field of light, where trees are autumn-
colored in the height of summer. At the river's bend,
a lone sculler pulls his oars across a surface
casting back no shadow of his face.
And coming from the hunt, a man with a rifle
balanced on his shoulder stops perplexed,
confronted by a fence.

               The river never moves,
the fish are caught in aspic,
and the woman's lacy figure
proffers blue spirea, orchids, frangipani,
which do not grow here.

OBSESSIVE REWORKINGS
OF THE SAME THEME

Blue sky, white snow, thin tracery
of branches. If I painted
I would seek a distillation

of these repeatable events, white sky,
blue snow, the quiet net the world constructs
to hold me in. I look out the window

which is frame enough, I take my hand,
warmer than the weather,
hold it against the glass.

The frost's thin tracery gives way
to the etched shadows of a tree on snow,
a blue stronger than midnight

against the peak of a neighbor's house.
I open the door to let the world in
and understand the true scope

of winter, not blue or white but blazing
in its own interior fire, a brightness
which has nothing to do with painting:

outside it's January, and it's cold.

LUST

· · · · · · · · · · · · · · · · · · ·

Once in a liquor store, stopped
at the end of an aisle, debating
what goes with lamb, I saw him. His eyes,

darker than I remembered,
flashed like the broken neck
of a bottle swiped on rock.

The day he bloodied my eye
in the schoolyard,
he hoisted me up,

and hanging by my jacket
from the cyclone fence,
I jerked as if a thousand volts

inflamed my brain.
I'd imagined him leaving
the shambles of that afternoon

to find an invisible job
alone in an oversized city
and I felt blessed

brooding over wine.
I'd been wrong about his future.
He would always stick out: like a pier

stretching its neck into deep water,
or a handgun hidden in a pocket
mistaken for the stiff outline of lust.

JAPANESE BEETLES

Every summer of my childhood
the old woman's roses
bent on their stems, heavy with beetles
who had settled near the pollen,

glints of carapace between the petals.
If I startled the flowers, the air
would fill with a polished mechanical
frenzy, a diaspora of insects,

so I moved with caution, dropping
the ones I picked in kerosene
until the metal can I carried blazed
with beetles. She paid

a dime a dozen; when I was sick
with fumes and greed I'd hurry
to her bedside for my prize. But God has
"an inordinate fondness for beetles,"

and thirty years from then, this summer
in my garden, they've eaten their way
through everything in sight.
When I walk the rows, a haze

like August heat rises, a whir of wings
leaves a frail green lace in its wake.
The flowers I cut are poorer for their visit;
a zinnia still captures in its petals

the oriental green, the iridescent brown
of an earthly shell. This one I have
is silent, will not fly away.
It shines. It burns in my hand.

MUSIC

Upstairs the Chinese man with his violin
plays the tortured music of the deaf.
It's Monday morning. The sun
streams across the off-white coverlet.
I think of him standing before the page
littered with dots and stems, the curious
calligraphy of sound he doesn't hear,
scraping the tail of a horse
across the strings.
I stand, yawn, stretch,
and in the kitchen, light a flame
under the kettle. At the smell of coffee
drifting through the floorboards, he puts
down his bow and I too stand
in the stunned silence
none of the other senses fills.

VAGRANT

· ·

He said he'd been the captain of a ship
stove in by the brute boned forehead of a whale

off Uapoa years before. He'd been abaft
at seven bells when he and all his men

were rocked like buoys by the blow, and water
filled the hold while over him the mainsail

turned to winding sheet. Five other men survived.
With them, he drifted weeks until they drew lots

from a pile of hand-carved splinters: being captain
pulled no rank with hunger. The taste of flesh,

he said . . . but who believed him? He was rescued
by a black Australian freighter, needed work.

Did we have anything to offer? Our small
midwestern town is miles from any ocean

and this man whose watery eyes were difficult
to fathom looked as though he'd never

seen a Frigidaire or combine. Where'd he come from,
some asylum? We're mostly farmers here.

We're businessmen who work hard, mind our business.
We attend our own, we weed our gardens.

Move on! we said. Get out of here! We don't like
lunatics and liars. He came again each evening

just at sundown, threading our quiet streets,
walking his witness. We finally took to leaving

scraps of pork and biscuits. When it became
less trouble to employ him than ignore him,

we said we needed a night watchman, though
we certainly had little enough to pay him.

That was years ago, of course. We hardly
remember life before him. He walks the blackened

streets and no dogs bark at him. Our children
come in willingly for supper and don't venture

out again. He wears the shirts and pants we once
were known for, we often mistake him for each other.

As we awake, the salt air touching us,
we hear his step outside our windows.

His measured tread assures us misery
is safely beyond our knowing. He has

a master key to all our houses. He carries
a flashlight we have paid for. And every hour

we hear a sound like breaking timber as he climbs
the spired steeple of our church and calls on us.

IN CANAAN

. . . .

My own ghosts travel with me when I come.
Sycamore and maple rustle in the sweaty dark,
the languid skin of a swimming pool glistens.
In backyard plots the gloss of peppers swells
to bursting, and the crickets will not quit

their sexual racket. Everywhere the moon
is breaking through. Behind their damask curtains
people watch the clouds' kaleidoscope
form hopes with words like *constant* and *betrayed,*
the pearls of rain run down the waxy magnolia.

I've been here once before, passed through
on the main street, forsythia and hemlock
whispering over the watered lawns, the winding
arms of turnabouts and driveways reaching to me
in the dark. Trees flowered, she wore

no underpants, the lace undid me. In the bedroom
were mirrors and barbells and silk
sheets on the bed. Downstairs I discovered
her parents, signed their guest register.
Outside two Dobermans stood guard.

I have come back to write my memoirs
with words like *nascent* and *disturbed:*
and *in that fabulous instant, all the days*
of my life fall down before me, begging
for mercy. I will give them none.

I have learned to be tough.
I hunger for the certainty
of truth, the unashamed reminder of the way
we started out as children, full of hope,
to end like this.

III.

READING

. . . .

They're slung like mannequins
among the pillows. Only the eyes
are moving, and a slightly moistened finger
flicking a page. They could be advertising
marriage: gold rings, identical, circle

equivalent fingers; her hand rises
from the quilt, hesitates, and lowers,
brushing his leg, a gesture so unconscious
it must mean their bodies belong partly

to each other. Still, they're centuries
apart: she's in Victorian London, he's
in hyperspace, and only in sleep's eccentric

fables are they more distinct. Tomorrow
after they rise and leave for work, a telephone

might join them; tonight nothing can.

DIGGING THE GRAVE

· ·

A light October frost dissolves
in the early sun, and the smoke our breath makes
wavers in rings, then disappears.
Under the firs it's still cold; the wind

rattles the lower cornfield and is gone.
Her mother moved here after the divorce
and Pleasantville—the vital losses.
This mountain marked the start of each departure

to camp or boarding school; it's close
as she can get to home, to where
one always comes to bury the dead.
At our feet her dog's stiff body lies

still wet from rain, and when she stoops
to pet her, running her hands
over the ribs, she can't yet find
the car that hit her. She arcs the pick ax,

I shovel out the dirt. The hole which grows
and darkens at our feet is emptiness
neither the body nor the mind can fill.
When she stood at her father's grave,

she saw the books he'd written as worthless
in this regard, the coded mysteries lost.
Now our exhalations vanish
in a silence she understands too well.

The pines echo, the stones accrue
more weight, the roots refuse . . . Admit it:
Death requires so little of the living,
taxing neither our capacity for love

nor language, only our backs, our confidence,
our expectations. There's so much false assurance
I could give her, but her pick hits bedrock.
There's no going deeper than this.

HINT OF SPRING

. . . .

At the turn of the year, into '84,
when the days succumbed to darkness
then struggled to return, everything broke

or so it seemed. The superstitious pipes
burst in thirteen places, ruining furniture
and books. The days were heavy with portents,

the sound of plaster being scraped off lath,
the noiseless warp of oak exposed to water.
Even the dog, panting in her pregnancy.

The night she burrowed beneath the bed,
she bore eight cellophane sacks and licked
them into life. The next day I came home

to find she'd tongued the last one's belly
so hard it had given way, and in my hand
I held just half a dog, just the trace

of its ribcage, thinner than bird bones,
and its two closed eyes. I thought of all
that water, eating away the foundation.

But today the air is blue as the hottest flames
which burnish our copper pots, and it smells
of dirt and hay. I rode the red bike you gave me

as fast as I could, turned the corner
by the iron bridge and tested myself flat out
against pavement and the brown-and-white dog

that raced me to a place where Indian Creek runs wide.
I came home, unable to catch my breath.
I can't describe the sun's

touch on my face. In a month the earth will burst
with daffodil and iris. Maybe we're coming through.
The world could almost maintain such happiness.

OLD FAITHFUL

. . . .

Not the jokes we told —*like selling*
the Brooklyn Bridge, plenty of ample parking —
not the stolid absorption of the crowds
trouping the concrete walkways to the crescent
benches; not even the young
mother slapping her children's knees
and elbows where bruises wouldn't show:

                when the first mineral-
saturated drops flew from their calcite entrapment
in a thunderhead of steam, when the stalagmite
of water inched higher, impossibly, supporting itself,
all distractions fell away —

                the aluminum buses, the smartly
cracking flags, nylon shorts, bear-proof garbage cans,
the careful hand-hewn plaques which warned
Unstable Ground, Boiling Water.

                In their wake, the flexing
muscle of the earth, oblivious to human attention,
its underground tension thrown
blistering into the sun-strewn air.

What was that throttle in my chest, that *sotto voce*
trembling in my throat? Last night as you slept,
I felt it again: this first husband you've just traveled
states to see, the sudden hot intrusion of the past,
the undomesticated weight of our three frailties,

forces at work which I can only sense.
In the dark there were no other tourists,
no signs to tell me which
of all the ground was safe, if any was.

HEAT LIGHTNING

· ·

Yes it's hot, so hot your forehead
sheens with sweat while neither of us moves.
You groan and ask for water, another cloth,
the slow relief of codeine falling
from a yellow pill. All summer you've been sick,

your body a hotel in which the virus
moved from room to room
searching for the perfect sleep. It seems
content now, lodged in the tympanum,
so all you hear is pain. I stand

and listen to you breathe until you're locked
in a dream where sound is tactile and your hands
move over the crumpled sheets, reading Braille.
What happens when the senses block? I want
to shake you, knock the virus loose, this slow

surrender to numbness, the sky's dull flash
and fade. Like a muffled bell, the clouds
are struck from within again, no sound. Thunder
is what I need, but tonight everything's quiet,
stifled by this heat. Are you still

breathing? When I hold my hand above your mouth,
the moist air worries my skin.
That front we're promised isn't moving in.
Just look at the night's dim pulse.

TORNADO WATCH

We're silent, driving insulates us.
The panhandle gathers storm clouds,
the horizon's fist. I'm so tense my voice
is intermittent static. It's there,

that spooky funnel touching the plains
and neither my fear nor the silence
changes that. Why won't you listen to me?
Why can't you pay attention to that looping

whirlpool sucking the dust of Texas
into its maw? Wherever we go these days
we argue in a circle whose center
I can't understand. When we stop for gas,

I take the question to the old man's
weathered singleness of jury. *Yep,*
he says. *It looks like that, it shorely do,*
but his corroboration is no triumph.

You men, you say, *you'll always stick
together.* Can our brief race's history explain
this wild intransigence? When I turn the radio on,
the male announcer drawls in Texan—dust

explosions, the price of feed in Hereford,
tornadoes rampant. I search the sides
for culverts, farm equipment, any shelter.
I want to get off this highway. I had such plans.

EVENING

• •

Evening is simple while the light's
still left, before the sun elongates
and the line we call horizon
dims, then disappears. Then night

becomes a screen on which regret
projects its haunting images.
The first time I slept with her
I traced the stamp of clothing

on her back, a map I thought I'd need
to find the future. When I rose
on my elbows, never had the next day
seemed so clear. When she left the final time

it was evening and I remember
paying attention to detail as though
I'd later be tested: a slice of moon,
the plane's twirling propellers,

a fresh crust of snow. Why memorize
the pattern of a chain-link fence?
I couldn't help it. Then one day I could.
I woke to find the sunlight on my face.

MARCONI STATION: SOUTH WELLFLEET

From this height and in this calm
we can see almost to Europe, and the waves
curl toward us like open parentheses, cupped fire
in their uncompleted curls. If ocean
is a word, like *month* or *year*, we use

to measure time, its slow erosion
of this cliff took longer
than the average life. Marconi built
four towers to send his invisible words,
and what remains crumbles back to sand.

All the ways I had of trying to talk.
I set fires on the dark plain, smoke
ascended in a vacuum the sky built. Tongue
twisted with dashes and dots, arms
like semaphores. Some days I was a ship

in distress, the wireless stuttered
mayday and the ocean drowned the call.
This need to speak out of myself
does nothing for the sun's dazzle
and spark, a rawness the season breeds.

North toward Truro, two boats
trawl the quiet water. Whatever we think
the wind steals away from us. But the waves
flash back, electromagnetic, a measured silence
where words aren't necessary, and the heart goes on.

IV.

STARS IN MAINE

Back where we came from
headlights and streetlamps
get in the way of the moon,
but here in the dark wind
off the freshly mown field
thousands of stars drift
across a deep black pool.

On Friday the cat drowned.
Pulled from the cistern, she lay
on the wet grass grimacing,
swimming in place. We buried her
on a knoll over the river, piled
rocks on her grave.

In the heavens the Big Dipper hangs
upside down, spilling
its weight of dead animals.
They scatter across the grave
of sky, bones falling apart
into stars.

It's dark up there,
another wilderness.
I can't connect the dots in the darkness,
can't find Orion to tell you
his sword is harmless,
you've nothing to fear.

BETWEEN TWO OCEANS

· ·

Once I saw in the aftermath of sun
a fleet of gilt-edged battleships
move south.

I stood by the Pacific,
waiting for a message.
I spent my days

deciphering nothing from the sky
and then the moon
like last night, barest hint of a smile.

Late fall, I walked in the marsh,
its splendid reeds broken by the wind,
and found a sea of milkweed. Pods

split in the cold air and a cloud of seeds,
a single breath, exploded before me. I've known
this generosity from total strangers,

heard love spoken by those I hardly knew,
their arms full of gifts.
Women numbed by the ice

they thought they loved, and men
who had forgotten childhood.
And all that water—

I have held it in my hands,
have failed to understand how it is nothing
without context. It mocks me,

both shield and mirror, until I am a boy again
at the attic window, watching storms move
over the Atlantic.

STOPPED IN MEMPHIS
· ·

Martin Luther King d. 1968

Rain battered the windshield
and the highway ran so deep, we pulled to the side,
hazards flashing. Other cars plowed on
across the Mississippi, but we forded

to this motel. Of course the storm
levitated. When I opened the plastic drapes,
slid back the thick glass doors,
hazy with condensation, and entered

the steaming afternoon the balcony offered,
it was almost as though nothing had happened.
In the motel's pool, a babble of kids,
a watery sun soaked in uneasy water.

By night the lights returned
and the TV told the news, no mention of storm.
Under the white blare of vapor lamps,
wraiths of steam rose from the parking lot.

It was eerie
being there. In the coffee shop
we ate without saying a word.
And that night I had a dream:

in water calm as a regular heartbeat,
the small boat journeys under a sky
so blue it allows no disruption
of travel, no assassin's bullet.

OUT HERE

In April, after winter's
left the ground, before the corn
has time to raise its green and inward-

turning shoots, out here
at night I can drive for miles
on a road potholed by frost

not having to decide
which way to turn, and sometimes see
another car move toward me

on this checkerboard the roads
divide to ownable squares:
when it's very dark—

no streetlights here, no moon—
I lose the earth, as though
the white Toyota floats above the asphalt,

otherworldly but benign.
I watch the other car assault
the intersection and I think

how easy it would be to touch
the gas more firmly, push the car
toward contact and tendrils of flame.

It's silent but for tires drumming
their monotonous momentum
while under the surrounding fields

seed corn lies in its yellow casings,
millions of kernels ticking in silence, waiting
to explode.

RING-NECKED PHEASANT

He appeared this afternoon, an apparition
waddling down the hill behind my house, an outsized
belly of a bird, lifting one scrawny leg
and then the other. I went outside

and watched his feathers magnify the light.
Oblivious at first, his brilliant head
jerking the barberry, he finally turned
a wall-eyed stare at me. I took a step

and stopped, and then another, as in a game
of Freeze, until I could have stroked him,
I was that close. Instead, I bullied him—
I see that now—flailing my arms. He stumbled

into air and sailed over the ridge, hitting the ground
a hundred yards away; the air rang with cries
so strident and alarmed, I felt ashamed.
He wouldn't return, I'd lost him through my bluster.

Or perhaps he'd come tomorrow—who could tell?—
hesitant as a child who knows the others taunt him
for no reason, no good reason at all,
and can do nothing but leave or try again.

ASPEN GROVE: NEW MEXICO

At that moment of twilight when elk
and deer are grazing, stripping
the groundward bark, we walk the fire road

as if we'd claimed this land, this stillness
after storm. The globed air smells of animal
and rain, so mountain-thin each breath

is concentration on the self. To the west
the sun outlines the peaks in blood,
each with its Spanish name, and thunders down,

still sovereign, on Los Alamos. From the porch
this afternoon we watched a mushrooming
hill of cumulus conquer the sky. We drank

imported beer and laughed as the rain
rattled the cabin's tin roof. We might
have been conquistadors ourselves. But here

hundreds of aspen rise as if the earth's
white hair were standing on end.
The untouched clearing

resonates with hooves, antlers,
a storm of mating.
We have not been visited by friends.

NAMING THE SHELLS

· · · · · · · · · · · · · · · · · · ·

Even the names we give them signify
our preference for the sturdiness of land,
as if our language could transform the alien:
sand dollar, acorn barnacles, sea grapes. In fact,

a man could wander months along this beach
and never find himself in seaweed
or in shell, and the waves constantly
changing the coastline are not similes,

but themselves. Each day the sea surrenders
a memory of what has eaten its green water,
spawned, been turned to sand. A channeled whelk,
a skate, a horseshoe crab, its barbed tail

a compass pointing north. Last week I found
a shark no longer than my arm, one eye
intact, and turquoise through its slit.
If I turned to the air for information

what would hear me? Could it tell me
sadness is a state these gulls
printing their hieroglyphs along the beach
have an awareness of, a need for,

that my house is built on rock, not sand?
These shells: false angel wing and razor clam.
This board. It could have been a bookcase
or a door, this glass a bottle or a window leasing sun.

SEALS IN THE DAMARISCOTTA

That spring I wanted a miracle
beyond the routine resurrection

nature grants each year,
a token of a human trait

beyond resilience. Let's face it:
I wanted love, a new beginning,

I wanted to erase my past.
As I walked toward the river,

among the riot of fall's dried weeds, the wind
amused itself, nattering in my ear, bothering

the sharp blades straining
through the ruin of that field.

I'm afraid I amused myself with ironies — *the more
things change* — oblivious to the fiddleheads

unfurling their sea-green music. My eyes insisted
on the possibility of woodchuck holes, in case

I had the opportunity to sprain
my fragile ankle, break my neck.

• • •

At field's end, the land fell sharply. Winter storms
had bitten off the bluff; below me, a wedge of sand,

then water. I saw acrimony everywhere
I looked — a bleached encrusted float

stranded for the duration, black remnants
of mussel shell cracked on rock, the abstract

spatterings of seagulls, and the half-moon
lunacy of jellyfish. Beyond all that,

out on the Damariscotta, the wind
played with the tops of waves, first flattering,

then knocking off their heads; the coy sun,
mesmerized by its reflection, flashed

in the pockets of the waves, a clarity
of constancy and change.

                    • • •

And out there in the midst of all that motion,
eight seals poked noses at the sun.

They barked. They barked. Sun beat
against their blackness like a wand.

After all these years, I can still feel
the blue-green globe they balanced, a world

away from me, can smell the fish
tossed from the bucket of the air,

their noses sleek and slippery as a promise.
Imagination holds the past in shimmering

relief, *what matters*, what makes darkness
bearable, a host of lights,

and lets the rest go. At dusk
a seal floats in the evening stars, applauding.

I BET

• • • • • • • • • • • • • • • • • • • •

You remember that night we sat on the deck,
a wrought iron railing enclosing us, serene
in our discontent? Above us, distress
was an old constellation, the stars
like far-away flares. You pointed to a spot
across the canyon, flicked your cigarette and said,

"I hate that light." I still don't know
why all our wits had narrowed to a point
of electricity among the oaks and pomegranate hedges
when, scattered above us, worlds were being born.
I know that I watched with you and ignored
the grey-green suede of olive trees,

the island scent of oleander, even the moonless
silhouette of horses in the orchard below us.
Sacramento burnished the western sky,
and yet we watched that light
and nursed our notions of bad faith. Your wife
was busy with her third-grade lesson plans,

and I remembered being eight and making
a shoebox scene of cavemen hunched over a fire.
Were even they unhappy with their lives?
We've traveled ages since their kindled warmth,
improved it so immensely that tomorrow
everything could finish in a flash. I bet

if it were suddenly expunged, you'd miss
that human light across the canyon,
only a speck, hardly enough to spoil
the hushed and darkened theater of the universe.
That night I didn't understand the starlight
we ignored had streamed across not only miles

but centuries; and here on earth, when it began
its flight, the Greeks who were inventing tragedy
must have looked up between the grey-green leaves
of olive trees to find *the bridge
outside of time,* our Milky Way, a light-strewn
path beyond all temporary pain.

PLUGGING IN THE FLOWERS

· ·

My own idea about whether or not to plug in the flowers
is somewhere between these ideas . . .
                              Donald Barthelme

1.
I have never plugged in the flowers
though this is the electric age.

2.
From the white petals
transparent as a mother's hands
flows the cord. A socket and a plug:
when they fit together lightning happens.
And the copper wires buzz
like bees in the flower's ear.

3.
Expectations: what can stop them?
More persistent than locusts
and more deadly, eating the new leaves
of the heart.

4.
If I gave you a daisy
would I give you a shock?

5.
Ask gravity.
A person will drop quick as a brick.
I would expect differently, a slow
floating down of the body, a current.

6.
If I plugged in the flowers
would light shine from my fingers,
would electrons
shoot from taut petals
into the darkness?

Would the borders of great avenues
glow in the night?
Would people not run off the road,
could I save lives?

If I plugged in the flowers,
could I plug in the trees?

ABOUT THE AUTHOR

Steven Bauer was educated at Trinity College and the University of Massachusetts. He is the author of the novel *Satyrday;* his articles and poems have appeared in a wide number of journals including *Antaeus, The Nation, North American Review,* and *Prairie Schooner,* which granted him the Strousse Award for Poetry in 1982. The recipient of fellowships from The Indiana Arts Commission, the Bread Loaf Writers' Conference, the Ossabaw Foundation, and the Provincetown Fine Arts Work Center, he currently lives in Bath, Indiana, and teaches at Miami University in Oxford, Ohio.

THE PEREGRINE SMITH POETRY SERIES

We are happy to add Steven Bauer's *Daylight Savings* as the third volume of the Peregrine Smith Poetry Series. Published as part of our promise to promote important literary expressions, we hope this book will contribute to the survival of literature's vital forms.

BOOKS IN THIS SERIES

Sequences by Leslie Norris
Stopping By Home by David Huddle
Daylight Savings by Steven Bauer